For the people who made me.

THIS GLITTERING REPUBLIC

QUENTON BAKER

Willow Books, a division of AQUARIUS PRESS

Detroit, Michigan

This Glittering Republic

Copyright © 2016 by Quenton Baker

Editor: Randall Horton
Cover photo: "One-room kitchenette" by Wayne Miller, 1947

ISBN 978-0-9971996-0-4
LCCN 2016957636
Willow Books, a Division of Aquarius Press
www.WillowLit.net

Willow Books Emerging Poets & Writers Series

Printed in the United States of America

Contents

what they bring your ass up in here for if you ain't gon'
tear shit up?

—FRED MOTEN

SAVED

Let us
all drink
to the sinkwater baptism
from whence I rise
                    (a nigger) loved by God.

A PARTY DOWN AT THE SQUARE

I looked & saw history caught
on a hinge, its two heads
like a seesaw rocking

A.B. Spellman

SURRENDER (sə′ ren·dər), *v.*

1. unavailable.

   e.g.:
   he was shotshe was shot   heshe was shot was shotwashot
   with her handsuphis   back   turned his handscuffed knee on
   her chest   what was thoughttobe   a gun
      a weapon   was actually a licensecellphonechild's   toy
   what police thought to be
      now reportedly car keys   a   grandjurydistric-
   tattorney decided tonight   ruled
      there was no wrong nowrongdoing   it was a
   goodshoot
      the police chief said tonight an internal investigation found
   no wrongnowrongdoing   the police were
      justifiedintheiruseof   justified in their use were
   justified it was
      justified force   shootingkilling 12yearold
   police were justifiedkilling
      the unarmed and she was unarmed the group was unarmed
   and surveillance footage
      has surfaced tonight twopriorconvictions   hewasunarmed
   but aggressively rushed
      the autopsy revealed thc in his   no angel   he was
   no altar boy nowwegoto donbackto aubreyinthestudio
   thankyouadifficultstory Coming up, a wild scene in India
   tonight: people were running for their lives as a leopard was
   on the loose!

JAZZ STANDARD

Thick lips grip the reed.
All toes tap.
Black bodies
lockstep with death.

The song is blood.
Broken time
kept by violent percussion.
Rifled out on balconies,
shotgunned in ballrooms,
pressed like oil
onto sidewalks,
slow curving roads.

MUSEUM OF MAN
for Sara Baartman

A dark theme keeps me here
with you, Sara,
in this museum of man.

I am your big-dicked son,
your big-assed daughter:
public pool body,
playground,
metro transit body;
shitty inheritance
for rough, white hands.

Some days I'm tall as God's hairline,
full of dark like good sex.
Other days I'm tall like a hanged thief,
brown as your buried child.

There will never be a moon
or season free from the heritage
of your harvested skeleton —
but you're more than dismemberment
aren't you?

Men fucked you, wanted
to lick the elongated labia
of the missing link.
Men fucked you, wanted
to own freedom, wanted
their wind to sit in the collar-mark of a martyr.

Continents away from tribe and Eastern Cape,
you put own-voice on public record:
I'm content to make my money
on the streets.

I won't save you, Sara.
And I won't place a cup
on the ridge of your ass.

May I sit with you?

Will you tell me about your river,
your love,

the small ways we say no?

BETWEEN

I am matter.
I cannot disappear,
dissolve.
I merely suffer a transfer
from triumph to tyranny,
sightline to shadow,
poured from the drooping corners
of a smile to the scowl's hard line.

Mask to mask.

DAMIAN TURNER

We are dirty, dark breaks
in the long bypass of evening.

I am here every night.

To give loss a name is homage,
to think it only has one name is sin.

What is the price of a bullet in Chicago?
What is the King's English
when the most common full stop
comes before a caliber?

DRIP
for George Stinney, Jr.

It's a fine spring day.
Not too hot, no rain.
Two scoops
of Alcolu's finest sweet cream
just for you, little man.

Take your time
enjoy the fat chill
of each lick
and don't let nobody rush you.
Don't matter if you finish
before it starts to melt.
Let the sugary expansion
run an opal river
down the dark bed
of your small arm.
Let it fall *tiptiptip*
to the stone floor
little man
like a milky deluge
and you, the little black god
of sweet cream rain
blessing the valley beneath you.

SURRENDER (sə' ren·dər), *n.*

2.   A lie told to a child.

   e.g.:
   Hands outside   bang.
   before he steps from the cruiser   bang.
   shrink yourself   bang.
   do everything she says   bang.
   like this. Watch: bang.
   no that's too fast—   bang.
   No that's too slow—   bang.
   Your speed was good

   but your mannerism: bang.

   too black   bang.
   Stop crying   bang.
   It's too aggressive

                                   bang.

                                   bang.

                                        bang. bang. bang. bang.
bang.

bang.

      bang.

MEET ME DOWN AT THE SQUARE

the couple holding hands in front of Thomas Shipp and Abram Smith

They gonna swing   I swear
if he dies   them niggers gonna swing
and I can't wait to see you   I can't wait for after.
Pale skin   lavender smell   sweet sweat.
I wanna stick underneath
your bluewhite speckled dress.
You my best girl my best girl
I put forever inside of you
and I can't wait for everyone to see   the broad belly
building our child.
I cant stop.
I wanna put as much of me as I can fit
I wanna chew up the waddling dusk
coax it down your throat.
I want your fat, perfect belly to blot out the sun.

If he dies   them niggers gonna swing
so meet me down at the square.
I wanna push up behind you
smell the pine in your hair
feel yours and mine   guzzle and grow
toward this world it deserves.

DAILY NEWS

No aneurysm in the pipeline.
Uninterrupted
fresh   black   sludge pumps wild
through the fat fountain.
Bound black scum yawns
out from sopping mouth.

Get dirty   get paid
in a newold kind of wet.

MARY TURNER

Her Talk Enraged Them
           —Savannah Morning News, 20 May 1918

You never know how thick   empty can get
until it's on you.

Until you lift up acres
of untilled, abandoned fields
hold them upside down
and ask the fat weeds that fall out   for a story.

It is the story of a woman   black and reaching.

Mary is twenty-one,
eight months pregnant
though her face belies any weakness
from the moon she's swallowed.

Her man just been folded into branchweight,
caught in a wide sweep
launched by another nigger's etiquette breach.
Now   full of grief and baby,
she goes calling for warrants.
Black and public,
Mary yells for names on receipts,
trying to fix in her mind
          what justice look like.

This also the story of men   white and sodden

wet like only settlers can get

                          dripping from the deep dive
of putting niggers in an ocean of dirt.
                          They the names Mary wants.
                          They settlers
                          they discoverers.
She run.   They settle. They discover her.
On the Sabbath at noon,

19

they take her to a quiet bridge
for a history lesson.

Settler record say: we own where we make landfall.

In this cloister   sanctum for string-up
Mary hangs by her ankles.

Settler record say: the moment we touch begins inhabitance.

Oil   gasoline
turn her clothes skin   to sport.

Settler record say: be still   be our peace and stay live.

But Mary done provoked
and now her body is barely a body
rather flesh made frontier
made borderland   made supply line
made trading post.

Settler record say: we revise colony with powder/good metal.

So they redraw Mary with a hog-splitting blade,
shape her into a primer
on what it look like
when a black woman speak.

RENDERED
for bodies in streets

You bullets, be edict!
You blood, be sanction!
There is a kneeling
in every spill of it,
in every spurt: a signing.

I deem this pavement promissory,
I accept the kill
as signature,

now leave him.
Let the ink mature.

SURRENDER (sə′ ren·dər), *n.*

3. An accepted offer;
   a ritual;
   shamanic speech;
   lit sage able to clean
   the threat of me.

   A posture
   to make a human
   appear in the mind
   turn demon into pedestrian,
   lover,
   fellow trialist.

   e.g.:

CLEAR LAKE AT THE BOTTOM OF THE BELLY

open me up the me of me
put it inside where i need
let me carry it around
all day

ELOUISE LOFTIN

I (aI), *pron.*

Minor gods tell me I is through,
say it's run gold medal heat
and won. Now needs icebath/
quiet time.

Minor gods tell me: I is gauche.
We are post-discovery.

Minor gods tell me:
get I out your poem.
Transcend.

i tell minor gods:
your I cast wide shadow.
i was and am that umbra.

Your I authenticated with god blood,
separated by torque from king,
civilized, history. My i popped out
when lights came on
and nigger hit the floor, dropped,
not cool to be held anymore.

When i sit still,
my body breaks apart—
tenderized and torn
by the I i haven't been.

i in my head infects,
ingrown, pulped against the Mississippi
the killing rage, the silence.

In the worst wreck of my inner space
there is a note: go to the page.
And i return to the i's like mine:
precious, partially-crushed,
and we lend shape to one another
in this glittering republic.

CORNER STORE AND BACK AGAIN

I wake up well enough to wash dishes,
use my fingers for something new
besides knitting disease.
Fingernails bathe and break
in bloodwarm water.

Afterward, I walk to the corner store for a re-up—
ain't no medication like self-medication
'cause self-medication don't stop—
on the way back, seventeen steps
in front of my dishpan body:
a screech, a honk, the silence
of fast-moving metal in the wrong place;
a chronic-depression-gray Volvo
brutalizes itself against a tree,
sent there by a red light runner,
no doubt in the most important of hurries.

Some poor white lady pushed through the windshield,
frozen like God pressed pause on Law & Order.
Cell phones flip and slide, fingers swipe themselves
toward 9-1-1.
White faces crowd around the gap-toothed wreck;
gathering is their shaman maneuver.

I dip—
my shaman maneuver—
brown bag held with two for safety,
slide past the huddled,
the gawking, the helpful;
hearing my momma's voice:
boy, you know better than to be around
when the po-lice show up.

I feel like shit
for picking right now
to not forget
so I pray for that white lady's blood
jumping
down into the radiator.

A NIGGER, THIRTEEN WAYS

1.
A
new presence. The barely drawn edges of an
I. Brown
gristle puffed with
griot soul, an
etched heart that will strain to imprint itself on
rough steel.

2.
Accelerated progress through elementary school
No other child matches his dexterous
intelligence or his
ground cumin skin. Thank you
God for his mother's hustler spirit. She sought out the entrance
exam into the program that would tell the teachers:
relax, you can expect something out of *this* one.

3.
A
new girlfriend.
I love you, I say (right?)
girlfriend says: *I love you too.*
Girlfriend says: *my dad is home, so you can just drop me off. It's
easier.* Word, I say. *He
really isn't open-minded like me,* she says.

4.
*Ay
nigga:
I'm for real: every
gotdamn day this Chinese nigga be trippin on me
gettin on my fuckin nerves
eying me and shit thinkin I'm stealin his greezy-ass fried
rice*— *nigga, fuck ya buffet.*

5.
Abaddon. He's biblical.
Never got into mythology but

26

I'm cool with Abaddon.
Greek mythology I mean,
Greek. That's like the only one right?
Except
Roman. Right?

6.
Aaron S.;
nice kid.
I tutored him after school in math,
gave him my
graphing calculator at the
end of the semester.
Respect the polynomials, I said.

7.
Ambidextrous motherfucker
nice with the rock.
Inside game mostly but would step out
get you with the jumper or hesitate, head fake
go to the rack smooth
easy left-hand layup
ringing off the glass.

8.
Amazing Grace or
Nobody Knows the Trouble I've Seen or
I'm on My Way to Canaan or
Go Down Moses or
Get Away Jordan or
Every Time I Feel the Spirit or
Roll Jordan, Roll or

9.
"America land of opportunity mirages and camouflages"
        "speaking loudly sayin'
nothin' you confusin' me you losin' me your game is twisted
        want me enlisted
in your usury" "reflection rarely seen across the surface
        of the lookin'
glass walkin' the street wondering who they be lookin' past
        lookin'

gassed" "I find it distressin there's never no inbetween we
either niggas or kings we either bitches or queens the daily
ritual seems immersed in the perverse"

10.
At YMCA summer camp
near Lake Chelan
I won the watermelon eating contest; the
girls liked how the hot-ass sun hit my skinny sixpack, the
guys liked that I could
eat a huge fucking watermelon
really, really fast.

11.
Alcoholic.
Never met him but
I was told he held me once
grinned, even. Rare. Only have the one picture of him
got it restored and blown up last year around
Easter: he's young, sitting on the steps
reading, his own son between his legs.

12.
At least. At least. It's a mantra.
No hard feelings. I mean
I loved him. I mean, I love him. Monday through Friday:
gone. Saturday and Sunday:
gone, but a different kind.
Escaped? No. Absent? No.
Reluctant, maybe, but flesh, at least.

13.
Ammunition is something I've hidden from but
never lacked. Out of habit, I thumb bullet after bullet
into my chest. My ribcage is a drum magazine
girding a heart of etched
glass. I am afraid
every day, because I am also the barrel, the firing pin, the
reticle, the frame, the trigger.

HOLY AND BLACK

The moving figure of God casts the shadow
that grows the toenails in my socks,
the shadow the barn owl walks upon
like Jesus on a dark lake.
On the decorations in a nigger cemetery,
God casts the shadow that cradles the glass,
the metal, the broken pots.
On the wet 3 AM curb, while stoplights dump
leftover greens and reds,
the shadow speaks.
Some hear tyranny—
You are holy,
I hear the shadow say.

God casts a shadow on the branches
and spit stuck in my thick naps,
and on the day I decide to become small, to fit in this world
I will shave my head of its holiness
and keep the clippings as a relic of myself.

ST PETER'S CHURCHGOERS STARE AT THE YOUNG BROTHER COMING HOME FROM A SATURDAY NIGHT WALKING ACROSS THE STREET AND RAPPING TO HIMSELF

You call him some racist shit,
some ignorant shit.
You point and say: that's the one the sirens come for.

You translate the jangling language the empty flask speaks
to the brass that buttons his back pocket as sin talk.
You think his 7AM stumble across your arrival
is a willful toetap to death rhythms.
You smell the liquor poisoning his pores
 and believe him prodigal.

You feel the headboard slap
in the sweat-made grooves of his naps
and clutch your daughters' arms,
and in that noble intent to protect
you miss the seraph playing fugue
on his harpsichord heart,
you miss the goosebumps jumping his skin in this,
his moment of modest creation —
a melodic prayer thick with failure you impose
and grace you did not think to recognize.

God is in him
black as the ever-expanding backhand of the universe.
The Devil is around him
banging deep on the boy's tom-tom skull,
and the brother is   begging
for words that fit.

SELF-PORTRAIT

Watch. I'll take a selfie. It'll look like
eclipse, like

a wretch wrestling the dark.
Really watch though.
Expect to connect to me.

Don't let your
yearning drift
inside the reasons for my casket.
Need me alive. Put your greed toward
gathering breath into my failing lungs

because air is hard to come by here, shoved
underneath and pressed between every brick, avenue
thoroughfare.

Whisper or wail, I work
even the tiniest vibration against this

dynastic rule for
one reason:
no one gets
tired of forgetting. So I

heave what's left
against
violence,
erasure. Now,

tear open the long bag of shadow.
Offer yourself to me.

INVERSION

I am space.
Black without shape;
confinement's interruption.
Rejoice in this,
it is the first step.

I am cold-shouldered time,
misused spirit made chattel,
crude ballast.
I cannot be buried—
I carry the sunset in my mouth.

Put your lips to mine now.
Drink deeply.

TRANSIENT

Some [stars] are there but some burned out
ten thousand years ago....You see memories.
                    —Anne Carson

We built gods
          real slick-smooth
big god-looks
          on that stage
big god-breath
          big god-sweat
the bass pumped
          like priest-shrieks
like pure ghost
          had climbed up
in church hat
          in blue dress
the pews full
          but none sat
in god's house
          the fake dark
the track lights
          the sound man
he's drunk but
          we're gods
we built us
          this big sound
this black shit
          the trunk-thump
of raw truth
          we built us
we bang drums
          we sing loud
we're break beats
          we're *hands up!*
the whole crowd
          is white-faced
but who cares
          you paid ten
but so what

        your head nods
for my beats
        your arms up
for my words
        your drunk dap
for my fist
        your drunk lips
for my lips
        your scrunched fives
for my wax
        your drunk love
in drunk eyes
        for my swag
for my steez
        that I know
is dead light.

RETRIEVAL

We met in a storm drain, runoff
from some God-slick stone,
gathered by a busy wind and lucky slope.

I knew I'd seen your water before,
knew we'd been surplus together
prior to these throwaway bodies
yet still, we repeat the broken rhythms
of surviving:

How abyss are you? How blood?
How lung?
Can you human me
when my step is made demon?

How proxy am I?
How source? How willing?
When your body gets its answers,
can I remain the question
you remember from?

In darkness, under search,
we plot, break into each other
like veteran safecrackers.
Our climax: a hideout.

We were married at a die-in
for a thrownaway,
building toward retrieval.
I don't remember our vows,
just a woman
asking:
all this for one dead nigger?
Yes.
And I kissed you both.

LOVE LETTER

I live with the dark skin
of pleading just beneath my knee caps.
It spreads, the most loving virus.

Soon, my whole body
will be that rough skin
dry and pointless to touch.
I'll run from you.

I'll run
until I see a tall,
white stone building,

climb the stairs
until I reach the uppermost room.
You'll chase me,
calling my name.
I'll lock the door
so that you cannot follow.

I will jump,
and on the way down,
my skin will break apart
like an autumn canopy
and we can finally see
what holds it together.

CUL-DE-SAC

I carry the novelist, the poet,
the bled, the visionary.

I carry the schizophrenic, the nigger,
the conman, the prince.

I carry the placebo, the judge,
the holy grief of the broken-handled spigot.

My heart is a thick suburb.
There are empty rooms.

Come sit with me.

Let's behave well
beneath this tundra of stars,
freshly ridden in.

PUT TOGETHER

At a barely lit bar,   I   wait; vodka tonics
slow-sipped   will   hold me down.
3100 miles   always   far but never far like this.
Fever-stretched,   love   sick mongrels on stools at 11AM
no room to forget how   you   bend the world's edges to glass.

TORN APART

Your hips buck,	beautiful thickness;	I
turn liquid	about to spill.	*Don't,*
you pour	through a smile,	*think*
so much.	Your skin,	I
worship,	your touch	can love anything.

TRANSIENT
after Harryette Mullen

We talk without sayin nothin.
You told me if I came through,
you'd give me somethin.
                    —Method Man

    Weed bricks in the
living room. Couches on the
front porch. CD stacks in the
basement. *I love you.* Hallow-
een show bombs. I'm a doctor.
She's a nurse. Her hand up my
shirt. Still on stage. Cigarette
smoke. Pabst pissed into bushes.
Condom in the scrubs top.
Insomnia writes me. Gun in the
trunk. No bullets. Beat his ass
with a skateboard. Wet nights.
Downtown Portland. High Life.
$100 guarantee plus ticket sales.
Feather Man in the drunk tank.
Again. Indian Rights! Indian
Rights! White kid sent to buy a
beer at Pepino's. Liquor Con-
trol Commission fucked up the
Mexican homie. Stage sounds
thumped the strip. You're all
I need, says Radiohead nights
I can't sleep. Same song every
night. Same songs every show.
    Air mattress outside
San Diego. Rich white family
gave me bagels and lemonade.
Ain't thought in days. Sushi
on the beach. Dayquil chaser.
Prada sunglasses. Wannath-
rowupeverynight. *I love you.*
Apartment near the shore.
White dudes with dreadlocks.

Forgot to close the trunk. CD
boxes splashed the highway.
A tiny dog. Too thin hallways.
Everything dark in every club.
Low ceilings. Carpeted walls.
Love the bass hit. Gas station
parking lot. Old prostitutes
with open sores. Bulletholes on
a bicycle. PCP. Prison tats. He
called me loved one. 7 AM. Still
drunk. On the road to Mam-
moth Lakes. Whiskey Wednes-
day. Steak. Pasta. Making out in
the lobby. Handle of Jameson. *I
love you.* Crack vial in the snow.
Tweaked-out DJ. Hiding in the
fire escape. Middle of our set.
Wrong instrumental spinning.
He sleeps on coats, hoodies.
        Watching a car crash
in Sacramento. People dying
trapped in metal. *I love you.*
Drunk. Meth head in the hotel
room. Keeps saying the cold
water is hot. Half-empty Patron
bottles rolling on the van floor.
My laugh emptied out. Left the
Radiohead in Portland. Bleach
on my skin. Cut coke in the
green room. Miami driver's
license. Rolled up show flyers.
Went in to make a call, looking
for quiet. Crystal is a blonde.
Moon is a brunette. Bend,
Oregon. Mexican thugs beat the
shit out of this white dude on
a bike. Still had his helmet on.
Called the cops. Said it was a
nigger. Diamonds in his teeth.
Only two niggers in Bend. I'm
one. Drunk, driving over medi-

ans. Other one got an eighth in his backpack.

Walmart on Crenshaw boulevard. Not a single white face. Cell phone in my lap. Speakerphone rebels. Aliens live in Mt. Shasta. Travel in lava tubes. Too many people in one room. Praying in my head. *I love you.* New bottle of Dayquil. Claritin keeps my nose empty. Blackout drunk at the community center wedding. Hit on the groom's mom. Hung from the track light support beam, balanced on the monitors. Lemon Diesel in the corner of a trash bag. Obama's face on the inside of a bottlecap. Houndstooth blazer from Value Village. Sleeves too short. Home for the first time in months. She came in wearing a time machine. Turned the whole night into five years ago. Gave her my drink tickets. She didn't need 'em. I didn't stay. Tell me you'll feel the same way tomorrow. *I will,* she said. I will.

REVISION

I can't fuck with Marquez
too much magical misogyny
(the nigga writes rape manuals).
Can't fuck with Stein, with Stevens.

How can I get right
with the grandeur of your mind
when (at the zenith of power and mystery)
your only conjuration for me
was prop?

Don't give me that bullshit:
oh it's   just   a story.

Just.
What an easy word.

Like there's anything else.

Like we ain't   just   skin wrapped in and around story
tumbled from particular mouths.

Mine is nigger standard;
narrative loud as a Glock .40,
tilted: Love In The Time Of Extrajudicial Killing.

Science sick and incomplete:
String Theory: How The Noose Is America's Elementary Particle.

And all my wailing/my swagger/my dictates
on a destructive external reality
are margin notes, my nigga.

                        Edits.
                        Formulas.
Theorems related to the Hayes Principle
on how to make a human
                        out of a black wound.

LOVE LETTER

It's funny how much we ate—
we couldn't stop.
First dinner, then desert,
then the plates and the table.
At the show, she ate the stage,
I swallowed the microphones.
Back at the room we ate the chairs
the shower and the television.
Naked, breasts poised like the dark mystery
at the center of faith, she devoured the bed—
nothing left.

Behind her, arms around her victorious stomach,
I knew what it would take to fill us up.
Nothing short of a falling chunk of sun,
nuclear come to love us clean,
burn our shadow into the wall just like this.

DIGLOSSIC IN THE SECOND AMERICA

If you're kind, you say high or low. Honest: you say [default]
    or black.
But we don't say black. Not now. Only dog whistles:
    welfare queen
tough on crime. Wow! Look at her run, such a natural athlete.
What I mean is: two tongues: high and low speech; white teeth
    and suit or thug.
But don't I have both? Little mulatto codebreaker, identity
    that jump cuts like a running back.
Wait, am I even black? How black? On a scale of rapist
    to corner boy?

How black? What if I rapped, played ball and sold drugs?
But did it with white people? Judge: how black?
What I mean is: two countries. Binary. Between which lies
    the dialectic of my body.
Mixed body, both holy and fucked like the lowest temple
    prostitute.
I am you. Until the po-lice get called, then I'm sleeper cell
    felon.
Until the black cradle of rage rocks me. Then I've earned it.

Let's be clear: *it* is the bullet. Breakneck or steady, it comes.
    I deserve it.
How black is that? On a scale of home with family to
    mandatory minimum?
I love you. I'll kiss the ugly out your mouth, but will your lips
    cradle a permanent felon?
What I mean is: two Americas. One weight. Shaped from fear
    made reasonable. Justified.
I love you like I am you, like I've broken in front of you and
    you willed it remote. Exotic.
What I mean is: two Americas—binary—between which lies
    the dialectic of my body.

What I mean is: two Americas—binary—between which,
    lies have defined my body.
I am you. But my mother is white. How close to an oppressor
    do I sleep? Am I your enemy?

Sister light as hell. Three girls pull knives at the bus stop
       'cause she uppity.
Wait. Am I white? How white? On a scale of lacrosse to
       flashbang toss on a no-knock warrant?
How white? Do I love you or do I fuck you? Is it Gwendolyn
       or coon?
Am I extraordinary? Am I exempt? Am I negro to your nigger?

Can you trust me? Do I confuse your culture with poverty?
What you mean is: am I your enemy?
What you mean is: two Americas, one weight. Do I carry?
Do I know the safe black body is myth?
Will I let you be human or will I force your trauma?
Do I love you or sell you out?

What I mean is: I get you. And you. Two tongues,
       and each one makes sounds like danger.
Am I oppositional enough? Am I too oppositional?
Do I understand black shit? Do I only ever talk about black shit?
What I mean is: two Americas. One carries, one wonders
       what's so heavy
and is fascinated by the weight. And the grace.
What I mean is: we are lied to.

We are binary, are stuck,
are two Americas
vulgar alongside all these bodies— their hunchbacked silhouette.

MANDALA

All is vanity!
sayeth the tongue
inside my lover's lips.
Her mouth decriminalizes my geometry,
pours in me,
grain by grain,
the colored sand of patience.

Every inch of her is a path
leading to the center.
Where an image of a mountain
waits to swallow me;
a cup of blood,
waits to be tasted by my throat;
lips, housing a passionate tongue,
ache to share their pink prophecy .

EARLY

I was not,   (jet black, thrum of the interior
then I was.   offending silver, stab of velocity

Little, brown,
broken-footed seed   doctor snapped the caught leg
and what did I learn?   those months inside the blood?
crucially:
how to set breath to music   courage in the face of phantoms)

CALLING ALL PROPHETS

Today I am Ezekiel,
catching visions of the four-faced cherubim
rolling the beryl wheels within wheels
of God's throne.
I am eating the scroll of judgment
with a bull-bodied angel holding a knife
to my throat, going blind and dumb
in the name of faith
words of woe coating my teeth like raw honey.

God's throne zooms omnidirectional,
and I am compelled to follow.
Today's afternoon march
reveals the recluse sun to be a prophet as well.
She says: Be self-made! Find a way out!
You can be a victim or a staircase!
Climb! And dive past Heaven's sluice gate!
The tiniest sparrow, also a prophet,
says to the bird-bodied angels: you will die
an idolater's death!
The Institute of Divine Metaphysical Research says:
gimme your fucking money!

I am God's grenade pin.
Herald of explosion's ever-spreading edge.
It is my fate
to experience my fate
without really knowing it,
to spend my last breath saying:
oh.

NUDE TRANSFORMATION
after Yusef Komunyakaa

Is this how you imagined it?
Cecile smiles at my silence.
She walks to my bed,
vanilla scent in a purple blouse
and a knee-length black skirt
sculpted by her thighs.
Lamplight turns to moonlight
when it spills on her
unbuttoning fingers.
Her blouse falls behind her.

Do you think my breasts are made of ether?
She brings the sea and the dusk
in the switch of her hips.
I look at the floor.
Her slow walk toward my bed
turns hardwood to sand.
Her skirt litters the shore.

Is this where I keep my voodoo?
She slides her violet panties
halfway down her hips.
I avoid her eyes.
The rain outside is turning
from high hats to kick drums.

What is a bed but a sea to drown in?
I hear waves at my back.
She drops her unhooked bra
where the water meets the shore.

Tell me, what is it that you think I have?
That you want so badly now?
Her fingers are at my chest.

There are dark waters in me too, I say.
There's a setting sun in me, too,
and I want to wear my skin

as well as you wear yours.
She smiles again.

But you're afraid of me, aren't you?
She flicks off the moon.

LOVE LETTER

Dressed in the salvage of midnight,
we escape into new snow.

The devil has infiltrated our gin,
put the apartment walls on string
and pulled them tight to crush us.

Outside, my spirit still diabetic
with fear. I only remember to love
the fat-mouthed snow
when it falls on you.
In this moment, you've become
a hurdle of roses:
something to be clear of, to be caught in,
to be bled by, combined with.

I want your whisper by the fistful.

You are sacred
and I will not disengage my worship.
I am yours
from now until the acid
of God's bellyache.

LOVE (l⎅v), *v.*

1.   not   for
        you
        not   for
        you
        not   for
        you
        not   for
        you
        not   for   you
                                    not   for   you

           not for you

                                      not

                                      no

                       notforyounotforyounotforyounotfo-
ryounotforyou

        not
                for
                          you
not   for   you
                        not   for   you

not for

you,

        not   for   you,
                      nigga.

DIALECTIC

There is not in the world one single poor lynched bastard, one poor
tortured man [sic], in whom I am not also murdered and humiliated.
—Aimé Césaire

At the end of reason: the black saint of lynching.
　　　　There are torches at my feet, corkscrews in my chest.
　　　　My genitals, liver,
　　　　heart, kidneys become souvenir,
　　　　my flesh chunks in flame amid laughter.
　　　　Soot of my body plundered,
　　　　knuckles plucked and set on display
　　　　in department stores.

At the end of reason lies the torturer's line
　　　　fevered and spreading.
　　　　I have been in every set of eyes
　　　　seen what medicine torture can be.
　　　　The more you cut, the more you cut, the more you cut
　　　　the less human I must be.
　　　　But you were wrong.
　　　　You've birthed me
　　　　in my own blood
　　　　and nothing made you drag the knife harder
　　　　than my face turned mirror.
　　　　What gruesome ablution.

At the end of reason is our miserable debut,
　　　　a lack of recognition
　　　　the hollow-bodied limp
　　　　reciprocation died with.
　　　　We are human only if I see myself
　　　　in you and if you see yourself　　in me.

At the end of a different path, the sun warms
　　　　like whiskey
　　　　and freedom is meat in the mouth.
　　　　All we have here are the knife cuts.

At the end of reason, I am banished:
　　　　I, black head unfattened by shotgun shell, banished

I, black chest uncompressed by blue creased knee
I, black body unhunted, banished
I, black expectation deniggerized
I, black spirit decolonized, banished
I, black limb of the human paradigm, banished.

At the end of reason, I am locked in place:
I, criminal, locked in place
I, fat mouth, wet welfare lips, locked in place
I, Jezebel, locked in place
I, hyphenated sub-American,
I, natural athlete, locked in place
I, thug,
I, magical negro, locked in place
I, primitive golem of the earth,
I, Hottentot Venus,
I, Sweet Dick Willie,
I, tongue clicks in the bush, locked in place
I, godzilla to white women,
I, king gangster,
I, biological, locked in place
I, dark savage without spirit,
I, biological,
I, biological,
I, biological, locked in place.
I, flesh to be cut/maimed/forgotten
when it disobeys.
I deserve the shackle
deserve the whip, the noose.
I deserve the burning, the bullets, the bars.
I deserve solitary
because if I don't
what are you?

Acknowledgments

A sincere thank you to the editors of the following publications for giving these poems space in their pages:

Apogee, "Self-Portrait"
City Arts, "Giants"
Cura, "Dialectic"
Pacifica Literary Review, "Transient"
The New Guard, "A Nigger," "Nude Transformation"
The Seattle Review of Books, "Love Letter"
Vinyl, "Drip"

A big shoutout to Richard Owens of Punch Press for his incredible work on the chapbook, *Diglossic in the Second America,* in which several of these poems appeared.

About the Author

Quenton Baker is a poet and educator from Seattle. His current focus is the fact of blackness in American society. His work has appeared in *Vinyl, Apogee, Poetry Northwest, The James Franco Review, Cura* and in the anthologies *Measure for Measure: An Anthology of Poetic Meters* and *It Was Written: Poetry Inspired by Hip-Hop*. He has an MFA in Poetry from the University of Southern Maine and is a two-time Pushcart Prize nominee. Baker is a 2015-2016 Made at Hugo House fellow and the recipient of the 2016 James W. Ray Venture Project Award. He is also the author of the chapbook *Diglossic in the Second America* from Punch Press. *This Glittering Republic* is his first full-length collection.

CPSIA information can be obtained
at www.ICGtesting.com
Printed in the USA
LVOW10s0051151216
517339LV00001B/149/P